BELLY BUBBLE

Written & illustrated by Lottie Begg

Lemon Jelly Press
Isle of Wight UK
ISBN 978-1-9160214-5-7

Copyright © 2023 by Lottie Begg

All rights reserved.

No portion of this book may be reproduced in any form without written permission from the publisher or author, except as permitted by U.K. copyright law.

I think Mummy's in trouble, she has a big round bubble growing in her belly. I call it

BELLY BUBBLE

BELLY BUBBLE

is getting bigger every day...

BELLY BUBBLE

is taking up way too much space!

BELLY BUBBLE

is growing rounder and rounder...

BELLY BUBBLE

is taking over!

I am worried

BELLY BUBBLE

is going to...

What could possibly be inside the

BELLY BUBBLE?

A cushion?

A goldfish bowl?

A watermelon?

A bag of shopping?

NOPE!

None of those...

It turns out

BELLY BUBBLE

Was full of cuddles!

THE END

About the author

Lottie Begg is an author and illustrator based on the Isle of Wight. As a mum to four children the topic of pregnancy has come up time and again, but it wasn't until she misheard her daughter Josie say the word 'unbelievable' did 'Belly Bubble' come to life.

You can find more of her work, including illustrations and art work, at lemonjellypress.co.uk

www.ingramcontent.com/pod-product-compliance
Lightning Source LLC
Chambersburg PA
CBHW050747110526
44590CB00003B/107